THE BABY
John Burningham

D1345045

Jonathan Cape Thirty Bedford Square London

There is a baby

in our house

The baby makes a mess
with its food

We take it for rides
in the pram

Sometimes I help Mummy
bath the baby

The baby sleeps
in a cot

Sometimes I like
the baby

Sometimes I don't

It can't play
with me yet

I hope the baby

grows up soon

Little Books
by John Burningham

THE BABY

THE RABBIT

THE SCHOOL

THE SNOW

THE DOG

THE BLANKET

THE FRIEND

THE CUPBOARD